MW00720972

# THIS IS Maui

# THIS IS Maui

*Visions of the Islands*

# THIS IS Maui

*Visions of the Islands*

Photography by

**Douglas Peebles**

Mutual Publishing

Note: In the past, written Hawaiian language did not use macrons and glottal stops. The practice is generally accepted today as an aid to proper pronunciation and spelling. Diacritical markings as found in *Place Names of Hawaii* and in Pukui and Elbert's *Hawaiian Dictionary* have been added where appropriate.



ISBN-10: 1-56647-599-6
ISBN-13: 978-1-56647-599-0
Library of Congress Catalog Card Number: 2006921142

First Printing, April 2006
1 2 3 4 5 6 7 8 9

Mutual Publishing, LLC
1215 Center Street, Suite 210
Honolulu, Hawai'i 96816
Ph: 808-732-1709 / Fax: 808-734-4094
email: mutual@mutualpublishing.com
www.mutualpublishing.com

Printed in Korea

# INTRODUCTION

Maui, the second largest and youngest island in the Hawaiian archipelago, is home to a diverse population and a destination point for some of the most famous and wealthy people in the world. A contemporary oasis that offers top luxury resorts and spas as well as the pristine backdrop of a tropical paradise, Maui offers the balance between modernity and quaintness. For this reason, Maui has evolved into a culturally vibrant locale with something for everyone.

Artists and free spirits find inspiration in the natural beauty of their surroundings. Farmers and agricultural businesses cultivate fine Hawaiian coffees, sweet pineapples, Kula onions, even organic lavender in fields and fields of fertile land. Entrepreneurs envision Maui as a leading tech-center of the Islands. Despite the activities and ways that propel Maui towards further changes, the essence of Maui, fortunately, continues to remain true and eternal.

If you could float in the air high enough, you would see where Maui meets the sky. Island home of Haleakalā, a 10,000-foot temple that rises like an earth's chakra, Maui exudes not only the light of the sun from here but also majesty and spirituality, which is not surprising as Maui's namesake and birth are rooted in mythical legend. Named after Polynesia's well-admired Māui the demigod who pulled the Hawaiian Islands from the sea and harnessed the sun to slow its course and stretch out the day, Maui the island is a place that magnificently reflects nature's most creative, powerful, and breathtaking visage.

*This is Maui* blends the photographic talent of Douglas Peebles with the work of ancient chanters and literary giants whose words capture the magic of Maui. Along with the view from Haleakalā, and other famed sites on Maui, picturesque moments on Moloka'i and Lāna'i are also featured. As two of the smallest and least populated islands, Moloka'i and Lāna'i are often overlooked but always offer the most secluded and relaxing retreats and vacations. Whether you are familiar with these islands or admired them from afar, this photo album will reveal what few places on earth can do—inspire you to live in harmony with nature.

E komo mai a Maui nei, welcome to beloved Maui.

# From the Sky

. . . . . . . . . . . . . .

## Mā Ka Lani Iho

KAPALUA

# EAST MAUI

We were at the very top of the earth.

—Charles Warren Stoddard,
"House of the Sun" from *A Hawaiian Reader, Volume I*

‘Au i ke kai me he manu ala.

Cross the sea as a bird.
To sail across the sea.

Also applied to a hill that
juts out into the sea or
is seen from far out at sea.

—Hawaiian Proverb,
*‘Ōlelo No‘eau Hawaiian*
*Proverbs & Poetical Sayings*, 1983

MA‘ALAEA

POWER

MĀKENA BEACH

Mālia Hāna ke ahuwale nei Kaihuokala.

Hāna is calm, for Kaihuokala is clearly seen.

—Hawaiian Proverb,
*'Ōlelo No'eau Hawaiian Proverbs & Poetical Sayings*, 1983

HĀNA COAST

# LAHAINA

Pa ka makani, o ka Moaʻe,
hele ka lepo o Kahoʻolawe i Māʻalaea.

When the Moaʻe wind blows,
the dust of Kahoʻolawe goes toward Māʻalaea.

—Hawaiian Proverb,
*ʻŌlelo Noʻeau Hawaiian Proverbs & Poetical Sayings,* 1983

# KĀʻANAPALI

# HOUSE OF THE SUN

. . . . . . . . . . . . . . .

## HALEAKALĀ

# HALEAKALĀ

We were far above the
currents that girdle the lower
earth. We lived and breathed
in cloudland. All our pictures
were of vapor; our surroundings changed continually.
Forests laced with frost;
silvery, silent seas; shore
of agate and of pearl; blue,
shadow caverns; mountains
of light, dissolving and rising
again transfigured in glorious
resurrection, the sun tinging
them with infinite color.

—Charles Warren Stoddard,
"House of the Sun" from
*A Hawaiian Reader, Volume I*

Akāka wale o Haleakalā.

Haleakalā stands
in full view.

Said of anything that
is very obvious or
clearly understood.

—Hawaiian Proverb,
*'Ōlelo No'eau Hawaiian*
*Proverbs & Poetical Sayings*, 1983

# HALEAKALĀ

Haleakalā has a message of
beauty and wonder for the
human soul that cannot be
delivered by proxy.

—Jack London,
"The House of the Sun" from
*The Spell of Hawaii*



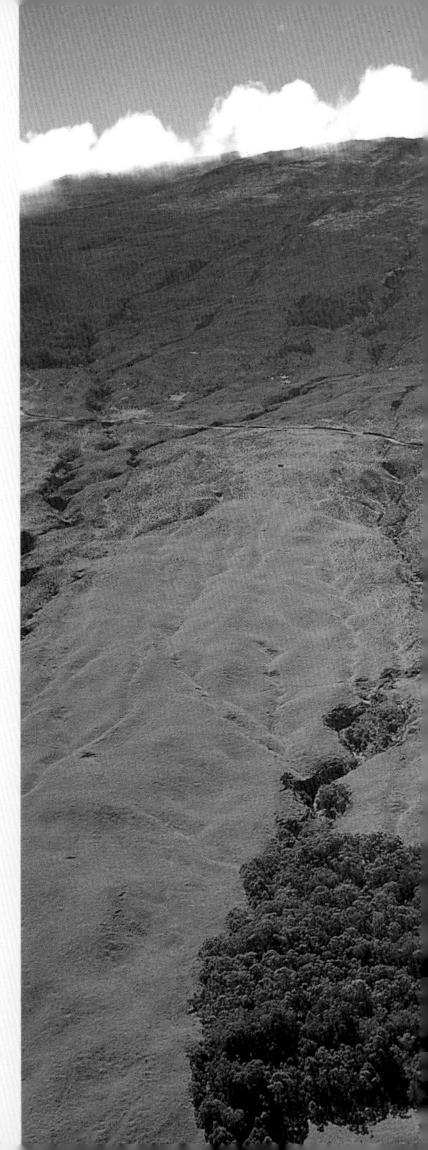

# Countryside

. . . . . . . . . . . . . . .

## Kuauli

Hāna Coast

KAPALUA PINEAPPLE FIELDS

Na pali kinikini o Kahakuloa.

The multitudinous cliffs of Kahakuloa.

—Hawaiian Proverb,
*'Ōlelo No'eau Hawaiian Proverbs & Poetical Sayings*, 1983

TARO GROWING IN HĀNA

KING PROTEA

PUKALANI

Ka makani kāʻili aloha o Kīpahulu.

The love-snatching wind of Kīpahulu.

A woman of Kīpahulu, Maui, listened to the entreaties of a man from Oʻahu and left her husband and children to go with him to his home island. Her husband missed her very much and grieved. He mentioned his grief to a kahuna skilled in hana aloha sorcery, who told the man to find a container with a lid. The man was told to talk into it, telling of his love for his wife. Then the kahuna uttered an incantation into the container, closed it, and hurled it into the sea. The wife was fishing one morning at Kālia, Oʻahu, when she saw a container floating on a wave. She picked it up and opened it, whereupon a great longing possessed her to go home. She walked until she found a canoe to take her to Maui.

—Hawaiian Proverb,
*ʻŌlelo Noʻeau Hawaiian Proverbs & Poetical Sayings,* 1983

Moe kokolo ka uahi
o Kula, he Hau.

The smoke of Kula
traveled low and swift, borne
by the Hau wind.

Said of one who is swift
in movement. Also, in love
and war much depends on
swiftness and subtlety.

—Hawaiian Proverb,
*ʻŌlelo Noʻeau Hawaiian
Proverbs & Poetical Sayings,* 1983

# WATERFALLS

. . . . . . . . . . . . . . .

# NĀ WAILELE

Ka ua Laniha'aha'a o Hāna.

The Rain-of-the-low-sky of Hāna.

Refers to Hāna, Maui. Once, the young warrior chief Ka'eokulani ran to a banana grove to escape a sudden squall. As he stood safe and dry in the shelter of the banana leaves he lifted his spear. It accidentally pierced through the leaves and a trickle of water came through. He remarked that the sky where he stood was so low he had pierced it.

—Hawaiian Proverb,
*'Ōlelo No'eau Hawaiian Proverbs & Poetical Sayings*, 1983

# HĀNA COAST

WAIMOKU FALLS, KĪPAHULU

And such a ride! Falling water was everywhere. We rode above the clouds, under the clouds, and through the clouds! And every now and then a shaft of sunshine penetrated like a searchlight to the depths yawning beneath us, or flashed upon some pinnacle of the crater rim thousands of feet above. At every turn of the trail a waterfall or a dozen waterfalls, leaping hundreds of feet through the air, burst upon our vision.

—Jack London,
"The House of the Sun" from
*The Spell of Hawaii*

# Rising Peaks

## Nā Pali

ʻĪAO VALLEY

WEST MAUI MOUNTAINS

Ka pali kāohi kumu ali'i o 'Īao.

The cliff of 'Īao that embraces the chiefly sources.

'Īao, Maui, was the burial place of many chiefs
of high rank who were the ancestors of living chiefs.

—Hawaiian Proverb,
*'Ōlelo No'eau Hawaiian Proverbs & Poetical Sayings*, 1983

Mahalo
WHALE MIST

Keikei Lahaina
i ka ua Pa'ūpuli.

Majestic Lahaina in
the Pa'ūpuli rain.

—Hawaiian Proverb,
*'Ōlelo No'eau Hawaiian
Proverbs & Poetical Sayings*, 1983

At our first night's camp, in
the Keanae Gulch, we counted
thirty-two waterfalls from a
single viewpoint.
The vegetation ran riot over
that wild land. There were
forests of koa and kolea trees,
and candlenut trees;
and then there were the trees
called ohia-ai, which bore red
mountain apples, mellow
and juicy and most
excellent to eat.
Wild bananas grew
everywhere, clinging to the
sides of the gorges…and over
the forest surged a sea of
green life, the climbers and a
thousand varieties.

—Jack London,
"The House of the Sun" from
*The Spell of Hawaii*

KE'ANAE PENINSULA

# A Day at the Beach

## He Lā Ma Kahakai

KĀ'ANAPALI BEACH

O Hāna ua lani haahaa,
ka ʻāina a ka ia iki i noho ai,
he ia na Kūʻula ma
laua o ʻAiʻai.

Hāna of the low-lying rain
cloud, the land where the
small fish is, the fish of the fish
god Kūʻula and ʻAiʻai.

—Hawaiian Proverb,
*ʻŌlelo Noʻeau Hawaiian*
*Proverbs & Poetical Sayings,* 1983

HĀMOA BEACH, HĀNA

WAILEA BEACH

49874

Mai ka lā hiki a ka lā kau.

From the sun's arrival to the sun's rest.

Said of a day, from sunrise to sunset.
This phrase is much used in prayers. Any mention of the setting of the sun was avoided in prayers for the sick; instead one referred to the sun's rest, thus suggesting rest and renewal rather than permanent departure.

—Hawaiian Proverb,
*'Ōlelo No'eau Hawaiian Proverbs & Poetical Sayings*, 1983

KA'ANAPALI BEACH

WAILEA

# KĪPAHULU

Ka Maʻaʻa wehe lau niu o Lele.

The Maʻaʻa wind that lifts the coco leaves of Lele.
Lele is the old name for Lahaina, Maui.

—Hawaiian Proverb,
*ʻŌlelo Noʻeau Hawaiian Proverbs & Poetical Sayings*, 1983

NĀPILI BAY, LAHAINA

KANAHĀ BEACH, KAHULUI

Aia nō i ke kō a ke au.

Whichever way
the current goes.

Time will tell.

—Hawaiian Proverb,
*ʻŌlelo Noʻeau Hawaiian Proverbs & Poetical Sayings,* 1983

WAIĀNAPANAPA

Malie o Maui, ua ahuwale ka ihu o ka la.

Maui is rainless, the nose of the sun is exposed.

—Hawaiian Proverb,
*'Ōlelo No'eau Hawaiian Proverbs & Poetical Sayings,* 1983

# Only on Maui

# Ma Maui Wale Nō

HUMPBACK WHALE

Ke kai holu o Kahului.

The swaying sea of Kahului.

Refers to Kahului, Maui.

—Hawaiian Proverb,
*'Ōlelo No'eau Hawaiian Proverbs & Poetical Sayings*, 1983

I puni ia ʻoe o Lānaʻi a i ʻike
ʻole ia Lānaʻi-Kaʻula me
Lānaʻi-Hale, ʻaʻohe no
ʻoe i ʻike ia Lānaʻi.

If you have gone around Lānaʻi,
and have not seen
Lānaʻi Kaʻula and Lānaʻi Hale,
you have not seen
all of Lānaʻi.

—Hawaiian Proverb,
*ʻŌlelo Noʻeau Hawaiian*
*Proverbs & Poetical Sayings*, 1983

LĀNAʻI

Wailuku i ka malu
he kuawa.

Wailuku in the shelter
of the valleys.
Wailuku, Maui, reposes
in the shelter of
the clouds and the valley.

—Hawaiian Proverb,
*'Ōlelo No'eau Hawaiian*
*Proverbs & Poetical Sayings,* 1983

HUMPBACK WHALE

# LĀNAʻI

Lāna'i a Kaululā'au.

Lāna'i of Kaululā'au.

Said in admiration of Lāna'i. Kaululā'au was a Maui chief banished to Lāna'i by his father for destroying his breadfruit grove. By trickery Kaululā'au destroyed the island's evil spirits and became its ruler.

—Hawaiian Proverb,
*'Ōlelo No'eau Hawaiian*
*Proverbs & Poetical Sayings*, 1983

# PROTEA

Pua ka uwahi o kā‘e‘a‘e‘a moku o Hina.

Up rose the smoke of the experts
of the island of Hina.

Said of the quickness of the athletes of Moloka‘i—
they were so fast that they smoked.

—Hawaiian Proverb,
*‘Ōlelo No‘eau Hawaiian*
*Proverbs & Poetical Sayings*, 1983

# MOLOKA‘I

Kūhela kāhela i
ka la'i o Lele.

Stretched out full-length
in the calm of Lele.

Said of a sleeper stretched out
in a careless manner.

—Hawaiian Proverb,
*'Ōlelo No'eau Hawaiian
Proverbs & Poetical Sayings*, 1983

LAHAINA

LUAHIWA PETROGLYPHS, LĀNAʻI

HĀKA‘A‘ANO, MOLOKA‘I

Maui no ka ʻoi.

Maui excels.

From the song of this title by
Reverend Samuel Kapū.

—Hawaiian Proverb,
*ʻŌlelo Noʻeau Hawaiian*
*Proverbs & Poetical Sayings*, 1983

MAUI

# Bibliography

Day, A. Grove, ed. *Spell of Hawaii.* Honolulu: Mutual Publishing, 1985.

Day, A. Grove, and Carl Stroven, eds. *A Hawaiian Reader, Volume I.* Honolulu: Mutual Publishing, 1968.

Pukui, Mary Kawena. *'Ōlelo No'eau: Hawaiian Proverbs & Poetical Sayings.* Honolulu: Bishop Museum Press Special Publication No. 71, 1983.